Zoom in on
RESPECT FOR
PROPERTY

Rita Santos

E | **Enslow Publishing**
101 W. 23rd Street
Suite 240
New York, NY 10011
USA

enslow.com

WORDS TO KNOW

borrow To use someone else's property with their permission.

citizen A member of a community.

civic virtues Behaviors or habits of citizens that are good for the whole community.

infrastructure Parts of a town, like roads and bridges.

maintain To care for something and keep it from breaking.

moral Good and right.

private property Something that belongs to one person.

public property Something that belongs to everyone in a community.

volunteer To do a job without pay.

CONTENTS

Our property is everything that belongs to us.

What Is Property?

Property is an object or place that people can own. There are two types of property: public and private. If you have a favorite stuffed animal, then that is your private property. It belongs to you. If someone else wants to touch it or play with it, they must ask you first. Public property is an object or place that is used by everyone in the community. Your local playground is public property. This means anyone can play there. But your bedroom is your private property and only people you invite can play there.

Good Citizens Respect Property

Respecting property is a civic virtue. "Civic" means having to do with the community. A virtue is an idea or behavior that is considered good and moral. So a civic virtue is an idea or behavior that is good for the whole community.

Taking care of public property helps the community.

By respecting property, we make our communities nicer places to live. When we respect public property, we do our best to keep it clean and fix it if it is broken. We respect private property by not using or taking things that don't belong to us.

Property Is Important

Property is important to people for lots of different reasons. Some reasons are easy for anyone to understand. For example, houses are important because they are where people live. They also cost a lot of money. Other reasons might only be clear to the owner. Sometimes, a certain toy

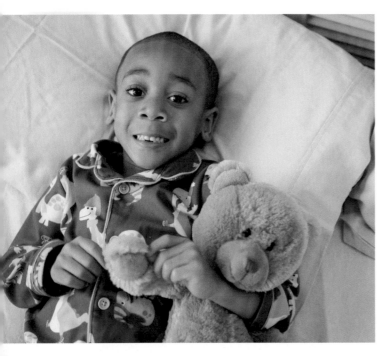

means a lot to you because it was given to you by someone important. It may not be expensive, but it has value to you. You should respect other people's property because something that might not be important to you could be very important to them.

Some of the things that we own are very special to us even if they are not worth a lot of money.

How Do We Respect Property?

You may have an outfit that you only wear on special occasions, like birthday parties or religious events. You take care of it by hanging it up carefully in your closet. When you wear it you might avoid activities during which you would get very dirty. By keeping your clothes clean, you are showing respect to your property.

Workers maintain public roads in order to keep cars and people safe.

How Communities Respect Property

Many towns show they respect property by paying to fix and maintain their infrastructure. Things like roads, bridges, and some buildings are town property that is known as infrastructure. If there are cracks or potholes in a road, the town will pay someone to repair them. Respecting our infrastructure makes our towns safer and nicer places to live.

Good Citizens Don't Steal

Sometimes people take property that doesn't belong to them. This is called stealing. Suppose a student takes a

Fast Fact

"Larceny" is a legal term for theft.

book from the school library without checking it out and never returns it. This is selfish because it means other students won't be able to enjoy the story. Also, the school library now has to pay to replace the book.

Sometimes people steal things because they are in need. A person who is starving might steal food in order to survive. If you are in a situation where you need to steal something to survive, talk to an adult you trust, like a teacher or police officer. They can get you the help you need without having to steal.

Shoplifting even a small item is wrong. It is bad for business as well as the community.

Respecting Property at School

Your classroom is made up of public and private property. Some things like books or art supplies are there for every student to use. Some things in the classroom, like your desk, may belong to you this year but will be someone else's property next year. Some kids like to write on their desks. That is a bad idea, because they have damaged the desk for the next student who uses it. By respecting school property, you can make school a better place for you and every student who comes after you.

The items in your classroom are often public property. It is important to take good care of them.

Respecting Our Friends' Property

When we visit our friends, we expect them to share their toys or games. Sharing makes play time more fun. You are probably careful with your friend's things because you don't want to break them. You know your friends would be upset if something happened to their property. If one of your friends was often careless with your things and broke a few of your toys, you probably wouldn't share with him anymore. This is because your friend was not respecting your property. When we borrow something from a friend, we should try to return it in the same condition. This is how we respect our friend's property.

> **Fast Fact**
> When you give something to someone for a short period of time, it's called a loan.

Fixing Things That Break

Accidents happen, and when they do we must try to fix them. What should you do if you accidentally break some else's property? The first thing you should do is apologize,

If you break a friend's toy, do your best to fix it or replace it.

then try to fix it. See if you and your friend can work together to figure out a solution. If you are unable to fix it, you should offer to replace it.

Citizens Respect Property

In many places, citizens ask their government to spend more money maintaining public property because it is valuable for everyone. Public places like parks and libraries give citizens somewhere to meet and bond as members of a community. When local governments invest in public property they are making sure that everyone has access to safe and clean spaces.

Free libraries like this one allow citizens in a community to lend and borrow books.

Citizens can also help maintain public property. You may like picking flowers in your mother's garden, but if you picked the flowers in the community garden, others wouldn't be able to enjoy them. When we visit public spaces, we should make sure to leave them as we found them.

Fast Fact
The largest park in the United States is Chugach Park in Anchorage, Alaska.

Keeping Our Communities Clean

Keeping our communities clean is a lot of work, but it's easy when we all do our part. Citizens can respect public places by cleaning up after themselves. When you have a

19

If everyone pitches in, it is easy to keep our communities safe and clean for all citizens.

picnic in the park, always remember to throw away your garbage before you leave. This helps make sure the park is just as nice for the next citizen who wants to use it as it was for you. Citizens can also help by volunteering in their communities. You can do your part by working in a community garden or helping to pick up litter.

When you take care of your friend's things, it shows you respect your friend. It lets her know that you care about things that are important to her. When we respect public property, it shows that we care about our fellow citizens. By taking care of public property, we can make sure that it can continue to be used by you and other people. You should take pride in your town's public property! As a citizen, it belongs to you and everyone you know.

When we care for public property like parks, everyone is able to enjoy them.

ACTIVITY: MAKE A PROPERTY POSTER

Now that you've learned the difference between public and private property, let's think of examples of each.

- Divide a piece of poster board into two sections. Label one side "public" and the other side "private."

- Look through old magazines, newspapers, or images from the internet for examples of public and private property.

- Cut or print out your images and glue or tape them to your poster on the correct side.

- Share your poster with your family or class. Discuss ways that you can show respect for each kind of property.

LEARN MORE

Books

Boritzer, Etan. *What Is Respect?* Los Angeles, CA: Veronica Lane Books, 2016.

Coan, Sharon. *Being a Good Citizen.* Huntington Beach, CA: Teacher Created Material, 2015.

Pegis, Jessica. *What Is Citizenship?* New York, NY: Crabtree Publishing Company, 2017.

Websites

The Constitution for Kids
Usconstitution.net/constkidsK
Learn the history of the United States Constitution and Bill of Rights.

Stories About Respect
freestoriesforkids.com/tales-for-kids/values-and-virtues/stories-about-respect
Read and listen to children's stories about respect.

INDEX

Published in 2019 by Enslow Publishing, LLC.
101 W. 23rd Street, Suite 240, New York, NY 10011

Copyright © 2019 by Enslow Publishing, LLC.
All rights reserved.

No part of this book may be reproduced by any means without the written permission of the publisher.

Library of Congress Cataloging-in-Publication Data

Names: Santos, Rita, author.
Title: Zoom in on respect for property / Rita Santos.
Description: New York : Enslow Publishing, 2019. | Series: Zoom in on civic virtues | Audience: K-4 |Includes bibliographical references and index.
Identifiers: LCCN 2017051442| ISBN 9780766097834 (library bound) | ISBN 9780766097841 (pbk.) | ISBN 9780766097858 (6 pack)
Subjects: LCSH: Respect—Juvenile literature. | Property—Juvenile literature. | Civics—Juvenile literature.
Classification: LCC BJ1533.R4 S26 2019 | DDC 179—dc23
LC record available at https://lccn.loc.gov/2017051442

Printed in the United States of America

To Our Readers: We have done our best to make sure all website addresses in this book were active and appropriate when we went to press. However, the author and the publisher have no control over and assume no liability for the material available on those websites or on any websites they may link to. Any comments or suggestions can be sent by e-mail to customerservice@enslow.com.

Photos Credits: Cover, p. 1 konstantinos69/Shutterstock.com; p. 4 Africa Studio/Shutterstock.com; p. 6 Joseph Sohm/Shutterstock.com; p. 8 Blend Images/Shutterstock.com; p. 10 Stockr/Shutterstock.com; p. 12 Fotosenmeer/Shutterstock.com; p. 14 OJO Images Ltd/Alamy Stock Photo; p. 16 AVAVA/Shutterstock.com; p. 18 EvgeniiAnd/Shutterstock.com; p. 20 Syda Productions/Shutterstock.com; p. 21 Anton Gvozdikov/Shutterstock.com; p. 23 Blend Images - KidStock/Brand X Pictures/Getty Images; illustrated houses pp. 2, 3, 22, back cover robuart/Shutterstock.com; illustrated children pp. 5, 9, 13, 17 brgfx/Shutterstock.com.